Feminine By Design

The Twelve Pillars of Biblical Womanhood

Feminine By Design

THE TWELVE PILLARS OF
BIBLICAL WOMANHOOD

BY: SCOTT T. BROWN

MERCHANT ADVENTURERS
WAKE FOREST, NORTH CAROLINA

Second Printing: September 2008

Merchant Adventurers, Inc.
3721 Quarry Rd Wake Forest North Carolina 27587
www.scottbrownonline.com

ISBN-10: 0-9820567-0-2
ISBN-13: 978-0-9820567-0-7

Book Design By David Edward Brown

Printed in the United States of America

The Finishing Grace of the Creation

"Woman was the finishing grace of the creation. Woman was the completeness of man's bliss in Paradise. Woman was the cause of sin and death to our world. The world was redeemed by the Seed of the woman. Woman is the mother of the human race. She is either our companion, counselor, and comforter in the pilgrimage of life; or she is our tempter, scourge, and destroyer. Our sweetest cup of earthly happiness or our bitterest draught of sorrow is mixed and administered by her hand. She not only renders smooth or rough our path to the grave, but helps or hinders our progress to immortality. In heaven we shall bless God for her aid in assisting us to reach that blissful state; or amidst the torments of unutterable woe in another region, we shall deplore the fatality of her influence..."

John Angell James, Female Piety, as quoted in Chapel Library's"
Free Grace Broadcaster, Issue, 196, Virtuous Womanhood

Table of Contents

PREFACE

For kingdom making and dominion taking women

The world needs Christ loving, husband helping, home making, dominion taking, kingdom making women.

The Bible not only teaches women to be possessors of gentle and quiet spirits, it also teaches them to exercise their God given wisdom and strength. They are vigorous and strong and distinctively feminine. They are supremely secure and are not frightened by any fear. They are brimming with confidence in the future and are not tossed to and fro by every wind of doctrine. They are happy because they fear the Lord and love His ways. Their worth is far above rubies, and they bring gain to their households. They are girded with strength and their clothing is of fine linen. The law of kindness is upon their lips. They do their husbands good all the days of their lives. They are *"pillars sculptured in palace style"* with adornments that radiate the beauty of Christ and diffuse the fragrance of the aroma of Christ in every place

(1 Peter 3:6; Proverbs 31; Psalm 144:12; 2 Corinthians 2:14-15). This book contains the stuff that makes women like this.

For my own daughters

In these pages you will find the scripture passages and the principles I attempted to teach my own daughters as I sought to *"bring them up in the training and admonition of the Lord"* (Ephesians 6:4). It lists the primary passages of scripture and outlines the conclusions I communicated to them from the time they were little girls. My hope was to fulfill the appeal of Jesus in the Garden of Gethsemane, *"Sanctify them by Your truth. Your word is truth"* (John 17:17).

A biblically faithful vision for womanhood

I wanted my daughters to have a clear vision of womanhood that did not arise from my personal understanding. I did not want it to spring from our family culture, nor did I want it to ascend from their personal inclinations and passions. And I definitely did not want it to be based on the cultural models around us. Because scripture is sufficient for all of life, their vision of womanhood had to be defined and limited by the very words of scripture so that they *"may be complete, thoroughly equipped for every good work."*(2 Timothy 3:17).

Culture at war with God

There are so many confusing and diabolical messages for young women today. Because every culture of the world is at war with God we must communicate to our daughters that if we follow the common culture, we will be embracing it's rebellion against God. This is why God commands us not to *"learn the way of the Gentiles,"* (Jeremiah 10:2) or to *"walk in the statutes of the nations"* (1 Kings 17:8), or to *"learn to follow the abominations of those nations"* (Deuteronomy 18:9) but to, *"be saved from this wicked and perverse generation"* (Acts 2:40).

Prepared for God ordained roles

I believe that daughters should be prepared from their youth to fulfill the biblical vision. They should honor the Lord their God by learning from Him and being satisfied in Him. He has designed rich and fulfilling roles for them and it would dishonor God and harm them to self-consciously mix the ways of the world with His ways. I encouraged my daughters to love His ways and cleave to His ways even though the voices of the world are always screaming for a different way. I would tell them that the ways of wisdom *are ways of pleasantness, and all her paths are peace. She is a tree of life to those who take hold of her, and happy are all who retain her"* (Proverbs 3:17-18).

Is biblical womanhood a relic of an ancient culture?

We live in an environment where many Christian parents and leaders act as if the words and phrases and principles in the Bible are simply relics of an ancient culture rather than a representation of the heart of God. This is why they see no problem with encouraging girls to spend their time doing things that have nothing to do with their biblically defined roles. I think this is a travesty against womanhood, against the family, against the church and the state. I would like to suggest that to train a daughter for something she has not been designed for or called to do (by God) is *"setting aside the command of God for the sake of your tradition"* (Matthew 15:3). This is why, in training my girls, I determined to train them only for what the Bible calls them to be and do. This is why I would not allow my daughters to train to be lawyers or politicians or corporate executives. None of these things seem to even come close to fulfilling the biblical vision of womanhood. Therefore I believed that it was wrong for me to cultivate desires for these things, even if my daughters seemed "gifted' in those areas or had a natural passion for them. Our daughters may be gifted in many areas, but they have been clearly appointed to a specific role in life.

The biblical limitations are liberations

Scripture does indeed place distinctive limitations on the roles of women and men. But, when it is God doing the limiting it is always a limitation that sets you free from the bondage of unworkable principles. It sets you free to be what you were created to be. It is God Himself who gives women particular roles and withholds others. As it is in the church *"All the members do not have the same function"* (Romans 12:4), so it is in all of nature including manhood and womanhood. In the same way, God has defined and limited the roles of women for His own glory.

Exercising freedom in Christ

For this reason, I was convinced before God that I was only free in Christ to train them to fulfill the biblical vision. Therefore, I was not free to teach them to be something other than what God established in scripture. As opportunities and desires for my girls surfaced, I would ask the question, "Does this explicitly fulfill the biblical vision for womanhood, or something else?" If it seemed to distract or contradict from the biblical vision it was excluded as an opportunity.

Consider the choices

Consider your choices in this matter. If you accept scripture alone you will have a perfect picture to use as your pattern. But, if you feel free to mix the principles of popular culture, your experience and your own wisdom, you can guarantee that you will facilitate a syncretized womanhood. The reality is, you can either have it God's way or you can have it your way. It is just that simple. If you believe that you can make up your personal version of manhood and womanhood as you go, you will end up with just that. But you must live with the fact that what you have is an idol of your own making. Re-inventing womanhood out of our own fallen brains produces a deformity of nature - a monster. This is why guiding daughters by scripture alone is the only rational position.

What should parents and daughters do about this?

First, they need to study scripture together. But this study needs to be governed by a heartfelt appreciation for the words and categories of scripture. Understanding requires humble and submissive hearts. Second, let me suggest that it is also critical that they memorize the scriptures that define their roles. With His Word in their hearts, they will be able to detect and expose the encroaching feminism. These activities will steady and embolden them when confronted with the feminist vision which pervades both church and secular culture. It will also make them wise in the things of God. Sadly, many churches are not upholding the biblical doctrine of womanhood, and they often unwittingly promote feminist ideology.

To clarify the biblical vision

This book is written to clarify the biblical vision. You will notice that I am assuming that the readers will someday be married. Although this may not be the case for every one of them, it will be the case for the majority. I hope it will be a helpful tool to prepare you to be either single or married for the glory of

God. For there is no better way to nurture them to fulfill the biblical vision for womanhood.

"Then God said, 'Let Us make man in Our image, according to Our likeness; let them have dominion over the fish of the sea, over the birds of the air, and over the cattle, over all the earth and over every creeping thing that creeps on the earth.' So God created man in His own image; in the image of God He created him; male and female He created them."

Genesis 1:26-27

Pillar 1
"An Image Bearer"

The breathtaking significance of womanhood is revealed in the Garden of Eden, in what appears to be the first poem in the Bible. God must have felt it was important to explain quickly that your dignity comes from heaven. Because of this, men are commanded to treat women with extreme care and to protect them to the death.

Blessed with valuable attributes

To be made in the image of God "Imago Dei" is to possess valuable attributes which are divinely endowed. As image bearers, women possess an immortal spirit, and are gifted with qualities that are reflective of God Himself. You have the capacity to know God and to be known. Therefore, you have an innate worth that demands thoughtful and special care.

What you believe about women matters

It matters greatly what you believe about the nature of a woman. The atheist believes that a woman is simply a random collection of atoms and you can do whatever you want with her - divorce her, abuse her, abandon her. It doesn't matter for she is only a random, meaningless collection of atoms.

The Hindu believes that women are a liability and their doctrine of womanhood gives men the freedom to despise and even kill them. For example, if your husband dies, you may be burned on his funeral pyre because you are viewed as a liability.

In Islam, women are viewed as property, to be used for pleasure and exploited for procreation.

If you are a female born in China, you may be killed at birth for you are not regarded as valuable to society. Males are judged to be of higher value than females.

In non Christian philosophies and religions of the world, women are devalued. But in striking contrast, Christianity places women in high honor. One way that God honors women is by surrounding them with protectors who are under specific commands to know, protect and nurture and even die for them (Deuteronomy 30, Ephesians 5:25. 6:1-4). Because of the forces at work in the world and in your own heart, you will often be faced with the temptation to think wrongly about yourself. You will perhaps even loathe your frame or your skin and be filled with discouragement.

In contrast, every daughter of Zion should marvel that she is made in the image of God. There are three radical life transforming implications of this for every daughter.

Joy and confidence

First, the knowledge of your nature should cause joy and confidence to fill your soul, for you have received your dignity and value from a source far beyond your own imagination and your culture. You are a completely unique creation for the glory of God. You were knit together in your mother's womb by the wisdom and knowledge of God. You lack nothing in value. Therefore, you must understand the wonder of your creation. You may get discouraged or even angry and end up thinking, "I'm not important." So remember that it is God, the creator of all there is who comes to you and affirms your significance. This was established before the foundation of the world, by the only wise God, who has anointed you with his own image.

Godly government

Second, this is one of the most important arguments for the godly government and care of your mind, body and emotions. Dear daughter of Zion, *"Possess your own vessel in sanctification and honor."* Preserve and keep it for the glory of God, by presenting *"Your body as a living sacrifice, holy and acceptable to God."* (1Thessalonians 4:4, 2 Timothy 2:21, Romans 12:1-2).

Don't despise God's guardianship

Third, don't despise the commands for the guardianship God has placed around you. Your nature as a woman is the reason God has built around you so many protections. As a young girl, God makes your father your head and charges him to govern you like

His Father in heaven does. When you are married, He places you under the safekeeping of your husband. If your husband dies, He provides your family and the church to care for you.

Since you bear the marks and attributes of the image of God, you have an appointment from God to live according to your design. You must play the role appointed. You are the specially designed daughter of the King of Kings.

"And the Lord God caused a deep sleep to fall on Adam, and he slept; and He took one of his ribs, and closed up the flesh in its place. Then the rib which the Lord God had taken from man He made into a woman, and He brought her to the man. And Adam said: "This is now bone of my bones and flesh of my flesh; she shall be called Woman, because she was taken out of Man."

Genesis 2:21-23

Pillar 2
"A Woman Not a Man"

As a woman, your gender is one of the beautiful expressions of the wisdom of God. It is the glory of God to array creation with diversity of form and function. He has crafted you with distinguishing qualities across a wide spectrum of physical and emotional attributes. These qualities exert a remarkable beauty and power in the world.

The creation order is significant

Genesis 2:21 is the first place in the Bible where we learn critical facts about womanhood. It shows the origin of woman; the sequence of the creation of man and woman; and it displays the distinction between man and woman. We will learn later in scripture that each of these elements is important in understanding the proper roles of womanhood. For example, the order of creation is important, *"for Adam was formed first"* (1 Timothy 2:13). This sequence and order of authority is proclaimed as the basis for the distinctive roles of man and woman, for God is *"the head of Christ, Christ is the head of man and man is the head of woman"* (1 Corinthians 11:3). To get any of these out of order is to rage against God's design. It would subvert the divine order to place man as the head of Christ, or a woman the head of God. In the same way, it is equally rebellious to place a woman over a man. For if it is lawful to put a woman over man, then it would follow that you could put man over God, or a woman over Christ.

This is a good point. [handwritten margin note]

The sinfulness of blurring the lines

It is sinful to blur the differences between men and women. The philosophy of androgyny insists that men and women are the same. They should be free to look the same, act the same, dress the same and pursue all the same things. Beware of those who would redraw the lines of masculinity and femininity (Deuteronomy 22:5). Beware of those who would put women in leadership over men in the church and in the state (1Timothy 2:11-13, I Corinthians 14:34, Isaiah 3:12, Exodus 18:21, Deuteronomy 1:13). Beware of those who would send women into combat (Deuteronomy 20:1-9; Numbers 31:25-27, Exodus 30:11,16, 1 Peter 3:7). Beware of those who would have women teaching the Word of God to men (1 Timothy 2:11-13, 1 Corinthians 14:34). Tragically, if you embrace this distorted vision of womanhood, you will lose your femininity, and be robbed of your distinctive beauty in creation. In so doing, you will withhold an aspect of the glory of God from your family, your church and your community. In addition, when women lead, it makes for weak men, powerless churches and dysfunctional governments. It is a sign of the judgment of God on a culture (Isaiah 3:12). Let's look at an illustration from Judges 4-5.

What about the leadership of Deborah?

Deborah lived in desperate times. She was a wise and godly woman in a time of spiritual darkness and social collapse. During that time she was judging the people who came to her. It was when men refused to lead, that she was pressured to lead the army into battle. Does this story justify women in leadership over men? A careful reading of the text gives us four crucial clues that show us that Deborah does not establish a pattern for women to follow. First, the story is NARRATIVE, which does not innovate or over ride established doctrine. Second, what was Deborah actually doing? She was judging at home under her own tree. She was not campaigning for leadership. She was accommodating not leading. She rebuked Barak for failing to lead. Third, the example of Deborah must be understood in the light commands and patterns of scripture which put men in leadership and women under protection (Exodus 18:21; Deuteronomy 1:13; 1 Corinthians 11:3; 1 Corinthians 14:34-35; 1 Timothy 2:11-14). Fourth, the story of Deborah does not promote equal opportunity to serve in leadership. It is a tragic depiction of when men disregard God, will not lead, and do what is *"right in their own eyes"* (Judges 21:25).

Distinctively feminine

God has wisely designed your womanhood to define your roles in this life. So, rejoice daughter of Zion, and be content in your femininity! When you think, act and dress in a distinctively feminine way, you will be declaring the glory of God. And, you will taste the happiness of having an inner confidence no one can take away. You will never have to wonder, "Why have I been born?" For the fact of your womanhood has explained a great deal of it. It is God who has made you distinctively feminine and your whole life will revolve around a uniquely feminine expression of the glory of God. While the world squeezes you into the image of a man, God liberates you to throw off the bondage and frees you to glory in your femininity. So as you walk through life, be aware of how important it is to bring glory to God through your peace and satisfaction for what God has ordained.

"Come to Me, all you who labor and are heavy laden, and I will give you rest. Take My yoke upon you and learn from Me, for I am gentle and lowly in heart, and you will find rest for your souls. For My yoke is easy and My burden is light."

Matthew 11:28-30

Pillar 3
"A Disciple of the Lord Jesus Christ"

Christianity has no praise for empty headed women, for it is the Lord Jesus Christ who makes women into lifetime learners. If they are faithful to Paul's command, *"let a woman learn"* (1 Timothy 2:11), and if they listen to Christ's appeal, *"learn from Me,"* they will be rich with the treasure that is more valuable than fine gold. They will be feeding on the best spiritual foods and refreshed by the clearest waters for mind and soul (Isaiah 55). Christ's women, are *"disciples,"* for He would fill their minds with knowledge that will satisfy their souls.

Happiness in Christ's discipleship

This is why daughters will find their greatest happiness when they are true disciples of the Lord Jesus

Christ. When you confess your sins, repent and believe in the Lord Jesus Christ, you will be saved and you will hunger for true food. This hunger will draw you to the feet of Christ to learn from Him. When you make Him your Chief Shepherd, you will find renewal for your mind and direction for your life through the discipleship of Christ. This discipleship is conducted through the devotion of your senses to Christ (Romans 10:9, John 3:16, 2 Corinthians 3:18, Romans 12:1-2, Hebrews 5:13-14).

Voices calling for discipleship

Everywhere around you there are wondrous voices that would call out to you to make you a disciple of the world. These discipleship voices come in the form of music, movies, books and friends. And if that is not enough, your own heart will take you there. And if you give your senses (eyes, ears and mind) to these disciple makers, they will make you into their images – guaranteed! No one can escape this principle of discipleship – we become like what we imbibe. We are made into the image of whatever we meditate on.

The lure of an eclectic life

The devil wants you to reach out into the world and eclectically create your own life any way you want – through your senses. The devil would make you free from all of Christ's commands, but it will not *"make you free indeed"* (John 8:32). Like your spiritual mother Eve, the serpent would like to lure you to embrace everything that seems pleasing to your senses. This will remove you from His blessings, and make you a disciple of the world which is passing away. This discipleship will *"kill, and to steal and to destroy"* the beauty God has in store for you (John 10:10).

Let the word of Christ dwell richly

So dear daughter of Zion, *"Do not love the world or the things in the world,"* for God has designed a much better and hopeful life for you (1 John 2:15). As a woman, you are created to nourish your soul on the words of the grace of God by heeding the voice of your master who says, *"learn from me."* These blessings are yours when you *"let the word of Christ dwell richly"* (Colossians 3:16). They are yours as you read scripture, *"When you sit in your house, when you walk by the way, when you lie down and when you rise up"*

(Deuteronomy 6:7). They are yours when you seek the Lord in prayer. And they are yours when you hear and obey the teaching of the Word of God in the church.

Christ your shepherd

In this way, Christ becomes your shepherd and you become His disciple. You will know the power of drawing your life from scripture. You will experience the confidence that comes by guiding your steps and living your life according to the *"Words of life"* (Philippians 2:16). You will be *"like a tree planted by rivers of water which brings forth it's fruit in season"* (Psalm 1).

"There is one body and one Spirit, just as you were called in one hope of your calling; one Lord, one faith, one baptism; one God and Father of all, who is above all, and through all, and in you all. But to each one of us grace was given according to the measure of Christ's gift."

Ephesians 4:4-6

Pillar 4
"A Member of the Church"

Christ is so kind that He plants His daughters in the fertile soil of the fellowship of the church, the body of Christ. In the church, Christ makes every daughter His bride, incorporates her as a member of His body, and places her as a living stone in His building (Ephesians 2:21). He has done this so that daughters would be nursed and strengthened there in His eternal family. This membership makes you a life long recipient of the wealth of the multiplied gifts of the spirit in this great, worldwide family of God (Ephesians 4:1-16, 1 Corinthians 12-14).

Delights of membership

As a member of the church, you can know the delights of membership in the body of Christ. These delights are explained in the *"one another"* statements in scripture which are summed up in the simple phrase, *"love one another"* (John 13:34). We live in a day and age where women say, "I must acquire a marketable skill in case my husband might die so I can take care of myself." In contrast, the Bible teaches that if a woman's husband dies and she has no one to care for her, the church is to care for her. As she is faithful to the church, the church will be faithful to her.

Temptations abound

But the evil one lurks to meet you in the church, to rob you of these blessings. For instead of a church member, the devil wants you to be cast out into a lonely world. He works to have you disconnected from the household of faith. To accomplish this he will have you misunderstand the importance of the church. Perhaps he will help you be busy with other things. Or he may tempt you to nurse displeasure in God's people. He is so vile that he will have you cultivate your disappointments in God's people into a spirit of rejection. He would even have you criticize the bride of Christ. He will have you withhold your love from her. He will have you deny your service to beautify her. He will have you make the church a low priority in life instead of a high priority. He will rob you of the very people who are most capable of loving and caring for you.

Enfolded in the people of God

While the devil wants to separate you from your spiritual brothers and sisters, God wants to enfold you in the people of God, *"Where it was said to them 'You are not My people', there they shall be called sons of the living God"* (Romans 9:26). There are enormous blessings awaiting you as you say with King David, *"I was glad when they said unto me, let us go into the house of the Lord"* (Psalm 122:1); And there are comforts for those who exclaim, *"One thing I have desired, that will I seek, that I may dwell in the house of the Lord all the days of my life, to behold the beauty of the Lord"* (Psalm 27:4). And there is peace for all who would conclude, *"For a day in your courts is better than a thousand elsewhere"* (Psalm 84:10). Your time is well spent as a willing volunteer as you offer your time, and treasure and energy for the members of the body of Christ. Blessings come down on the heads of those girls who would love the people and the elders and deacons and the songs and the scripture reading and the prayers and the meetings and the celebrations of the church of the Lord Jesus Christ. Involvement in the church should be one of the biggest priorities in a girls life. May you be *"like a green tree in the house of God, trusting in his mercy forever and ever"* (Psalm 52:8).

"Do not let your adornment be merely outward arranging the hair, wearing gold, or putting on fine apparel- rather let it be the hidden person of the heart, with the incorruptible beauty of a gentle and quiet spirit, which is very precious in the sight of God."

1 Peter 3:3-4

Pillar 5
"A Demonstration of Unfading Beauty"

There is no neglect of beauty in Christianity, for God would have the daughters of Zion be beautiful. There is no commendation in scripture for an unkempt, frumpy or dowdy appearance. Here in 1 Peter 3:3-4, Peter casts a vision for multifaceted beauty that is not merely outward. Consider God's desire that you would possess a deep unfading beauty that enhances outward appearance. In this way you will not be restricted by shallow outward beauty. Instead of becoming obsessed with appearance that passes away, He calls you to nurture what is eternal and precious.

Inward and outward beauty

In this way, Christianity argues for a beauty that is both inward and outward. And it is a modest beauty that does not flaunt either fashion or riches or sexuality.

A modest beauty

This is a beauty which adorns itself *"In modest apparel, with shamefacedness and sobriety"* (1Timothy 2:9). To dress modestly then, is to fulfill the principle of *"shamefacedness,"* which breeds a sense of humility and reserve that causes a woman to shrink from the boundaries. This stands in sharp contrast to the boldness and showiness that is often encouraged among women. One writer summarizes it this way, "Their dress will not say 'SEX!' or 'PRIDE!' or 'MONEY!', but rather 'purity', 'humility', and 'moderation'."

In contrast, the devil wants his daughters to be brazen, shallow, one sided girls, nurturing all of their affections on outward vanity. These girls are misled to think that their beauty comes from their appearances.

Comparing yourself with worldlings

If you find yourself appreciating and paying attention to the images of movie stars, music celebrities, and the people featured in teen magazines then you will be lured into investing your mind in a beauty that is only skin deep. No matter how nice many of these popular personalities are made to appear, they are going in a direction that makes for a hollow irrelevant dissatisfied existence. It is sad to find a daughter who is unhappy with the way God made her because she is comparing herself with worldlings. If you worry too much about every hair and piece of clothing, or are distraught about your appearance, then perhaps even your inner beauty is compromised and traded for the thin veil of appearance.

Beauty that shines for all eternity

How blessed it is to have a beauty that is both inward and outward and shines brightly for all eternity. In this way you can walk in confidence because you know the lie of outward beauty and the truth of real multifaceted beauty. This knowledge will keep you from being lured into it's hollowness. And this knowledge will help you to think clearly about yourself with a balanced view. And you know how to cultivate it, for it is at your fingertips. It is only God who opens the opportunity for a beauty that is deeper than skin. For the beauty of Christ upon you is not only outward, it is imperishable, creating in you an ever radiating inner beauty that cannot be extinguished.

"And the Lord God said, "It is not good that man should be alone; I will make him a helper comparable to him."

Genesis 2:18

Pillar 6
"A Helpmeet"

God designed women to be helpers, not leaders. This statement in Genesis 2:18, which makes them helpers, applies to all women. Some think the helping role applies only to married women. On the contrary, the Bible declares women to be helpers by nature, not only by marriage. This quality is part of her intrinsic constitution as a woman as Eve is the representative of all women - not just married women. In this way, a woman does not instantly become useful as a helper only when she gets married. She is a helper by nature, and a beneficial presence her whole life long.

In training to be a helpmeet

This means that parents need to specifically equip their daughters to play that role. The need for a helper assumes that a man is lacking something that a woman is able to provide. Perhaps this is why the woman was created after the man, from the man and for the man (1Corinthians 11:8). This is one facet of the glory of womanhood. Since you are an unmarried daughter in your father's house, you are not the helpmeet of your father, in the same way that your mother is, but you are in training to be a most excellent helpmeet. By helping your father and mother, you are learning to someday be the helper you were designed to be.

Set free for a powerful focus

This requires limitation, but by limiting the scope of your work, you are freed up to have a powerful focus. Think of the focus that we see in the woman mentioned in 1Timothy 5:3-14. She is not able to be a teacher of men or a leader or do everything that strikes her fancy, because she has her hands full of other valuable occupations. She displays piety at home, repays her parents, trusts in God, and continues in supplications and prayers night and day. She maintains blamelessness, is the wife of one man and is well reported for good works. She brings up children, lodges strangers, washes the feet of the saints, relieves the afflicted and diligently follows every good work. These qualities operating in her life before widowhood, qualify her for help if she ever becomes a widow.

The liberations of limitations

Notice how the limitations of womanhood actually set you free for activity in other areas. If she were a teacher of men or a leader (roles that have been withheld from her) she would not be able to function effectively in other areas. In this way, a woman who limits herself as a helper, loses nothing, but gains everything – even though she limits herself to the realm of the world of her home.

Dispersing your energies away from home

Instead of cultivating the patterns that would develop you into a beneficial helpmeet for your future husband, you will be tempted to disperse your energies everywhere else outside the home. Instead of cultivating a helping centered life at home, you will be helping everyone and everything else but home. This is not an argument against a life of helping others, for on the contrary, home life is designed by God as a center of help for others beyond the family.

Priority and focus

However, this *"helpmeet"* principle argues for priority and focus. God has not designed a woman to be the helper of every man, but only her own husband (Ephesians 5:22). In the same way, a daughter must learn the biblical principle of focus. The temptation is this: instead of a heart turned toward adding value to your father's house, and training yourself for this way of thinking, you could be inappropriately occupied outside the home, providing little help and producing little value for your family.

Why such a focused life?

Young ladies must understand why God would call women to a focused life. Here is one reason. A man's responsibility before God is so large that he cannot do his duty with his own strength. His duty is bigger than he is and it requires your participation. There is no way he is able to "take dominion" over the earth without your wisdom, your encouragement, your labor, your words, your ear and especially your affirmation. A man can endure and accomplish almost anything with the support and affirmation of a godly helper. This, daughter of Zion is how important you are. You can help create something wonderful by fulfilling your role as helper. And in doing so, you not only glorify God, but you come alongside God Himself to make a man more than he is on his own.

Precious days in your father's house

This is why your days in your father's house need to be days of preparation for a life of service - serving Christ by serving your father and your family. In doing so, you are fulfilling your divinely inspired role and preparing yourself for the future.

I pray that God would give us many women like Susannah Spurgeon who writes beautifully of her life as a helpmeet in this way,

"...my whole time and strength were given to advance my dear husband's welfare and happiness. I deemed it my joy and privilege to be ever at his side, accompanying him on many of his preaching journeys, nursing him in his occasional illnesses, his delighted companion during his holiday trips, always watching over and tending him with the enthusiasm and sympathy which my great love for him inspired. I mention this... simply that I may record my heartfelt gratitude to God that... I was permitted to encircle him with all the comforting care and tender affection which it was in a wife's power to bestow." [1]

---

1. (Charles Ray "The Life of Susannah Spurgeon," Edinburgh, The Banner of Truth Trust, 173)

"Wives, submit to your own husbands, as to the Lord. For the husband is head of the wife, as also Christ is head of the church; and He is the Savior of the body. Therefore, just as the Church is subject to Christ, so let the wives be to their own husbands in everything."

Ephesians 5:22-24

Pillar 7
"A Trustful and Submissive Wife"

This pillar brings us to the inner workings of spiritual power in the heart of a woman. A woman's strength and stateliness is governed by her humility and confidence in the sovereign hand of God. This is the ground of all submission and the peace that flows from it. Every girl should realize that God has designed home life as a training ground to equip her to cultivate a trustful and submissive spirit. By cultivating a spirit of submission you are concentrating spiritual strength. The beauty of this inner strength is that it prepares you to fulfill God's commands for women. For, *"God resists the proud but gives grace to the humble"* (1 Peter 5:5).

Embracing submission

As a young woman in your father's household, how would you embrace this spirit of trust and submission? What does it look like? First, you must realize that God has so arranged the world so that there would be authority and submission for the demonstration of the love of God that exists in the Trinity. The Son submits to the Father, the Father loves the Son and the Holy Spirit is deployed for service to mankind. Second, you must embrace the idea that God has not designed you as a woman to be a controller or a leader but a follower.

A right response to fatherly imperfections

Your confidence in God's sovereignty in submission often begins with trusting God for the father He has given you. Then it is tested when you are tempted to reject your father's counsel because of his various imperfections. If you exempt yourself from submission because of these imperfections in your father it will likely forge a tendency (in your disposition) to reject the counsels of your future husband.

The person you are becoming

The reality is, who you are now in your father's house, is the same person you are becoming. Many daughters lose their ability to respect and submit simply because they nourished rebellion as young girls in their father's houses. Often they withhold respect and submission because of their father's failures.

Becoming a submissive and humble woman puts you in the minority of women in this age. Women today are being trained for independence, leadership, distrust and rebellion, not submission. Instead of cultivating the marks of a trustful and submissive wife, you will be inclined to claim your independence and throw off authority as early as possible. This happens when you are hard for your father to lead. It also happens when you make it hard for your father to protect you.

Heart check

You will find that a dishonorable and un-submissive spirit begins subtly in the heart. As a young girl, you will most likely be tempted to belittle or even despise the directions of your father. If you are doing this in your heart, you are in grave danger, because these patterns will follow you all the days of your life. When honor is lost, so is a good future (Ephesians 6:1-3). If you do not break these patterns, they will break you. In times like these, the wisdom of Solomon is needed, for he says *"Give me your heart"* (Proverbs 23:24).

The Pattern can be broken

It is the blessing and glory of God that the pattern can be broken as you acknowledge your sin and repent of any rebellion that might be brewing in your heart. But by nurturing a trustful and submissive spirit, while still in your father's house, you will become an inspiration to all in your household. In doing so, you will learn to submit to your father. This will prepare you to submit to your own husband someday. Your learning to walk in humility now as a young woman will make you into a source of grace and harmony throughout your life. In learning how to submit, you will be securing many happy and productive hours for your family and your church.

"Admonish the young women to love their husbands, to love their children, to be discreet, chaste, homemakers, good, obedient to their own husbands, that the word of God may not be blasphemed."

Titus 2:5

Pillar 8
"A Keeper at Home"

Titus 2:5 says that a woman's focus away from home causes the Word of God to be blasphemed. Why? The woman who neglects ruling and nurturing her home leaves everyone in a vulnerable position. Bad things happen at home when her energies are directed elsewhere. This is why it is so striking that there is no one quite so marginalized as the keeper at home.

The mocking of keepers at home

Those who choose to be keepers at home will be mocked and belittled. They will be made to feel guilty. They are scolded that they are wasting their lives. They are told they are not making quite enough of themselves.

Keepers away from home

Why is there such a pressure? The reason is that the world would have women's lives cause the Word of God to be blasphemed. They do this by becoming keepers AWAY from home. But God has command-ed that women be keepers AT home, *"that the word of God may not be blasphemed."* With something so important at stake (blasphemy) it is no wonder that homemaking is so viciously attacked, so casually undervalued and so easily dismissed. But, in Titus 2:5, we learn exactly what the older women should be teaching the younger women - how to be *"keep-ers at home."* Apparently, even in the ancient world, younger women needed to be taught how to do this, for it did not come naturally enough. Things have not changed much.

Un-protected homes

You must understand motivation behind the hate-ful wiles of the devil against homemaking. The roar-ing lion is seeking to destroy the souls of the next generation. He prefers unprotected homes. Instead of ruling and nurturing their homes, they are ruling and nurturing elsewhere. This is where women get their impulses to invest their time and emotions in things outside the home. In this way, women leave their homes unprotected.

Barren homes

Women whose feet wander from home make homes barren and stark. They may be tempted to think that some kind of ministry is worthy to pull them from a homeward life. But we must evaluate and unmask these allurements for what they are. They are often diversions from the world, ready to steal what is beautiful from you and your children. And, they cause the Word of God to be blasphemed. Instead of a keeper at home the devil wants you to spend your energies on everything outside the home. Interestingly enough, in our day of internet communications, a woman can "travel" far from home, and have her heart elsewhere, even though she might be sitting in her house.

A wise woman builds her house

The beauty and power of home life is hard to overestimate when a *"wise woman builds her house"* (Proverbs 14:1). She builds investment and beauty and stability that would make a family say, "There's no place like home." God has appointed a home to be a center of the ministry of the church; a source of peace for all who enter there; a place of hospitality. The home is the fountain of society, and the spring from which flows the members of the church, the ranks of business and the citizens of the realm.

Filling the earth with worshipers

Please understand how important home life really is. O daughters of Zion, see what a piece of heaven you can provide to the weary and lost of this world by making your home a rich and overflowing fountain of the love of Christ. See the importance of a rich home life that sends out happy children to the ends of the earth. See how being a keeper at home makes you a key player in raising the next generation. Understand how you will be filling the earth with worshippers and providing the churches and towns and nations with the knowledge of God.

"Who can find a virtuous wife? For her worth is far above rubies. The heart of her husband safely trusts her; so he will have no lack of gain. She does him good and not evil all the days of her life. She seeks wool and flax, and willingly works with her hands. She is like the merchant ships, she brings her food from afar. She also rises while it is yet night, and provides food for her household, and a portion for her maidservants. She considers a field and buys it; from her profits she plants a vineyard. She girds herself with strength, and strengthens her arms. She perceives that her merchandise is good, and her lamp does not go out by night. She stretches out her hands to the distaff, and her hand holds the spindle. She extends her hand to the poor, yes, she reaches out her hands to the needy. She is not afraid of snow for her household, for all her household is clothed with scarlet. She makes tapestry for herself; her clothing is fine linen and purple. Her husband is known in the gates, when he sits among the elders of the land. She makes linen garments and sells them, and supplies sashes for the merchants. Strength and honor are her clothing; she shall rejoice in time to come. She opens her mouth with wisdom, and on her tongue is the law of kindness. She watches over the ways of her household, and does not eat the bread of idleness. Her children rise up and call her blessed; her husband also, and he praises her: "Many daughters have done well, but you excel them all." Charm is deceitful and beauty is passing, but a woman who fears the Lord, she shall be praised. Give her of the fruit of her hands, and let her own works praise her in the gates."

Proverbs 31:10-31

Pillar 9
"A Domestic Entrepreneur"

Proverbs 31 proves that keepers at home are not homebound, repressed, barefoot doormats. Rather, it portrays a woman full of vigor, commerce, relationships and productivity. She is the quintessential keeper at home. Her heart is upon prosperity for her husband. Far from being ornamental, she is looking out for opportunities for *"gain"* (Proverbs 31:11). Her industry and creativity foster the gain and profit of her husband's household. This is why her hands are always moving and her lamp does not go out at night. She knows real estate and agriculture. She promotes beauty in the clothing she designs for others and wears herself. She cares for hurting people in the community. She is a happy woman with a big life – providing for her family. Because her efforts are pointed homeward, we legitimately call her a domestic entrepreneur. Here, Lemuel's mother shows us a vivid picture of the outcome of a young girls training. She is a very valuable woman.

How women can strip a home of wealth

A woman whose energies are directed toward home is hard to find in today's world. Instead of encouraging DOMESTIC entrepreneurs, the world lures women away from home. This is how the home is stripped of it's wealth. In contrast, the Proverbs 31 woman makes her home a place of industry and investment.

Where it begins

How does this happen? It begins when you are a young girl, in the way that you think about your home. It is nurtured when you start to invest your gifts for your own gain, without respect for the gain of your father and the rest of the family. It starts innocently enough, but then becomes a pattern of life. Your energies are spent on the wrong priorities.

Builders and creators of family wealth

A girl should seek the answer to this question, "How do the activities that I desire, work for the building up of my home?" The answer to this question must begin with the recognition that a girl cannot do everything. For this reason, you must practice the discipline of focus on the things that build up your home. You do this by investing your energies and gifts and talents for the benefit of your home. This is the essence of a Proverbs 31 woman. In becoming like her, you become a giver, a builder and a creator of true wealth. And you will have children who rise up and praise you. This praise comes to you because you knew where to invest. Your home reflects the richness of your investment. Your accomplishments are evident and enduring. The women of the world may not praise you, but those who know you best find an upwelling of appreciation for the bountiful home life you created. For you were a woman who took the commands of God seriously and sought for the gain of your household.

"So God created man in His own image; in the image of God He created him; male and female He created them. Then God blessed them, and God said to them, "Be fruitful and multiply; fill the earth and subdue it; have dominion over the fish of the sea, over the birds of the air, and over every living thing that moves on the earth."

Genesis 1:27-28

Pillar 10
"A Fruitful Bearer Of Children"

The Bible says "have lots of babies." This message is proclaimed unequivocally and without any qualification everywhere the subject is mentioned in scripture. Whenever the Bible addresses having children, it always exalts fruitfulness and multiplication. When you find a monolithic message like this one, pay close attention, for the heart of God is being communicated in no uncertain terms. Therefore, God says, *"be fruitful and multiply"*, and *"multiply greatly"* because He desires *"godly seed"* (Genesis 9:1, Deuteronomy 6:3, Malachi 2:15) This is the only message that comes from scripture on this topic. This mandate to be fruitful and multiply explains another important dimension of your role as a woman. God calls you to think and live and pray and plan in such a way that you would contribute to the multiplied millions of worshipers before the throne of God from every tongue, tribe and nation for all eternity.

Liberated from children

In contrast, the popular voices of the modern age teach women to be liberated from the constraints of children. They teach women of the inconveniences and dangers of pregnancy. They preach the virtues of small families and the legitimacy of methods for controlling fertility. To achieve this they advocate the use of birth control and even the abortion of living babies.

Deflecting passionate appeals of scripture

Christian people may communicate the same underlying philosophy in gentler terms when they say, "God does not prohibit birth control" and "Get to know each other and have your career before you have children." In doing so, they deflect the passionate appeals, ignore the explicit uncompromising words and qualify the glowing praises of the Lord regarding children.

The unmixed message of scripture

This is one of the clearest doctrines in the Bible. God has made it plain that He desires His people to *"Be fruitful and multiply."* Those who do not respect the unmixed message of scripture are standing by to qualify or belittle the biblical message through their own personal opinions. Why? Perhaps it is this: instead of a fruitful bearer of children for the Lord Jesus Christ, the devil wants you to limit the number of mouths praising God on this earth.

Delighting in children

O daughter of Zion, God delights in those who love what He loves. It should be obvious enough that God loves motherhood and children. He has said that, *"children are a heritage from the Lord... a reward"* (Psalm 127:3-5).

A special appointment

God must delight in the exciting news that a child is growing inside one of His daughters. This calling to carry a baby is a very special calling. A husband is also called to *"be fruitful and multiply,"* but he does not participate in the process in such an intimate all consuming way. In this way, God has designed a woman to play an amazing role in fulfilling the mandate to be fruitful and multiply. May it be said of you that you knew the sweetness of embracing God's thoughts regarding pregnancy and childbirth. And that all those around you would rise up and say, *"Our sister, may you become the mother of thousands of ten thousands; and may your descendants possess the gates of those who hate them"* (Genesis 24:60).

"You shall teach them diligently to your children, and shall talk of them when you sit in your house, when you walk by the way, when you lie down, and when you rise up."

Deuteronomy 6:7

Pillar 11
"A Teacher of the Next Generation"

The Bible makes education a central occupation of womanhood. Contrary to most people's thinking about credentials and professionalism, God appoints every woman with children to be a teacher of the next generation. This means that women are deployed to one of the most important and exciting tasks given to any creature. As a mother, you step into a teacher's shoes. Daughters of Zion, God has given the primary responsibility for the teaching of children to parents (2 Timothy 3:15, Ephesians 6:1-4, Deuteronomy 6:1-9, Psalm 78:1-9). There is nowhere in scripture that indicates that teaching children is the responsibility of a government school system. Scripture is also clear that the Christian education of children is the primary responsibility of parents and not the church.

Christians don't outsource their children

Instead of playing the role as a teacher of the next generation, the great cultural voices want you to outsource the education of your children while you pursue your career, social status, ministry or hobby. This is an act of disobedience to the clear command of scripture. This disobedience has worked havoc in the rising generation.

A profound effect

Not only does this contribute to the downfall of both church and home, but it can have a profound effect on the woman herself. For when a woman throws off her God given teaching responsibility, not only does she find herself out of harmony with the design of God, her own learning and progress falters, and she becomes less and less knowledgeable.

Don't be robbed of the excitement of a child looking to you and asking the most important questions. And don't be defrauded of being the one who has the answers. Don't give up the personal growth and development and research and communication and organizational skills that come from being a teacher of the next generation.

A vision of disciplemaking

How inspiring it is to be included in the great divine discipleship vision which has come down from the *"Father of lights, from whom there is no variation or shadow of turning"* (James 1:17). In doing so, you will be preparing a people for God's own possession and pouring your life into eternal souls. You will be spending enormous amounts of time in one of the most important, intensive, personal discipleship enterprises on the planet.

"...the older women likewise... that they admonish the young women to love their husbands, to love their children, to be discreet, chaste, homemakers, good, obedient to their own husbands, that the word of God may not be blasphemed."

Titus 2:3-5

Pillar 12

"A Godly Mentor"

Where are the older women to mentor the younger? Unfortunately, these mentors have been stolen from the scene. This is a modern tragedy, for God's life cycle design for a woman is that she would begin life as a daughter, proceed to become a wife, then mother and grandmother, and finally a godly mentor of younger women.

Variation and texture to life

This is one of the ways that God provides variation and texture to a life that is ever changing. God has planned that someday, you would serve as counselor and guide to the younger women. Mature and earnest counselors are needed for those who are learning how to be true daughters of Zion. The church is full of young women who are being sanctified from their former lives.

The gift of a seasoned mentor

And God desires to give them a gift - a seasoned woman who will guide them to be chaste, to love their husbands and love their children. These women are *"teachers of good things."* This is not an official teaching position in the church (1 Timothy 2:11-12) but an informal, relational, one on one function. Her teaching is not designed to replace or reproduce the role of the elders.

Today creates tomorrow

Warning: if you do not so order your life now in preparation for this future life of godly service, you probably won't become this kind of godly woman. The danger is that by your priorities today, you may starve the church of this kind of woman tomorrow. Who can calculate the losses from this? But this we do know in our day, there are very few "Titus 2" women. Where are they? Here is the answer. They are not here because, in their youth, they neither had the vision or the preparation for this station in life. Be warned. This could become the story of your life. You may not finish well, because you did not begin well. This may happen to you because somewhere along the way, your first love was lost and you became involved in things that deprived you of the wisdom that fits this role. And many years later, the rising generation of women will be robbed of the counsels they so deeply need.

A lifetime of usefulness

God has designed a lifetime of meaningful roles and responsibilities for women. He has given you critical tasks throughout your life cycle. As you grow old, and the years of life increase your confidence in God, you become useful in a new way. Your fears subside and wisdom finds a rising foothold in your heart. God has done this so that you would have the capacity to bring blessing to the younger women. Your gray hairs are a witness to the distance you have traveled and the wise counsel that resides in your heart. All of these years have had a great purpose in the mind of God. He has been shaping you and buffeting you and giving you trials so that you might become a guide to the blind and a light to those who grope in the darkness.

A Final Word to Fathers

Exemplary fatherhood is demonstrated by the man who loves the heavenly vision of family life and takes decisive action to create it. As the head of his household, he creates conditions so that a daughter can become what God calls her to be. He has a little "wife in training" under his roof, who needs to become fit for her calling. It won't happen through osmosis. A father must rise up and protect his daughter through the knowledge of God.

The tragedy is that the world is so effective in upstaging a father and stealing what is beautiful and good from his daughter. The whispering lies of a false liberation are all around us. They cry "liberation, liberation," but there is no liberation. In nearly every corner of our culture, there is a cry for liberation.

Liberation from God's order for manhood and womanhood

Liberation from discipleship and worship

Liberation from femininity and modesty

Liberation from the church and relationship

Liberation from inner beauty and spiritual depth

Liberation from men and service

Liberation from submission and authority

Liberation from staying home and leading a quiet life

Liberation from childbearing and a multi-generational vision

Liberation from the bondage of teaching and personal discipleship of her children

Liberation from home centered work and production

Liberation from mentoring the younger women

In short, she may get "liberated" but she will also be stripped from all that God has declared to be beautiful and good.

She may get her way, but the way of the gospel will be compromised. For in time she will discover that this kind of liberation has nearly sterilized her. Her only protection from these things is to be *"Filled up with the knowledge of His will in all wisdom and spiritual understanding"* (Colossians 1:9).

Here is the crux of the matter. God has appointed fathers to protect their daughters through their personal presence and discipleship and communication of the knowledge of God.

"Through wisdom a house is built, and by understanding it is established; by knowledge the rooms are filled with all precious and pleasant riches. A wise man is strong, yes, a man of knowledge increases strength; for by wise counsel you will wage your own war, and in a multitude of counselors there is safety" (Proverbs 24:6).

Epilogue

Scripture indicates that the home is designed to be the central place where women glorify God. They do this through their obedience to the commands of God as they employ their gifts and fulfill their callings. Central to their calling is to be *"a helper suitable"* (Genesis 2:18).

Why then are we training our daughters toward a career outside the home? Why are we sending their hearts and affections in a different direction? What if we instead trained our daughters to fulfill the biblical role of helper to a husband? What if we trained them to be helpmeets? What if we truly trusted in the biblical pattern for our girls and deliberately prepared them for that and that alone?

"Is your heart overcome by fears of "what if?"

"What if she doesn't get married?"
"What if she has a passion for…?"
"What if her husband dies?"

When asking these questions we should remember that since the days of Adam and Eve, God has taken care of mankind's fears and "what if's. He has made provision for His people through the promises in His Word. We must trust His instructions all the while remembering that He *shall supply all your needs according to His riches in glory*" (Philippians 4:19).

It is for us to train our daughters after God's glorious design! It is for us to help them love the way of a woman! It is for us to help them be fully prepared to be a blessing to a husband as a *"helper suitable."*

Deborah Brown